The Art Of
Civil Litigation

A Behind The Scenes Look At A Real Trial Lawyer

Daryoosh Khashayar, Esq.

Speakeasy Publishing
73-03 Bell Blvd, #10
Oakland Gardens, NY 11364
www.speakeasypublishinginc.com

Ordering Information:

Quantity sales. Special discounts are available on quantity purchases by corporations, associations, and others. For details, contact the publisher at the address above.

Orders by U.S. trade bookstores and wholesalers. Please contact Speakeasy Publishing: Tel: (888) 991-2766 or visit www.speakeasypublishinginc.com.

Printed in the United States of America.

Published in 2017.

ISBN: 978-1-946481-38-2

DEDICATION

This book is dedicated to my brother Koorosh Khashayar who has been and continues to be the inspiration in what I do and how I move forward

in my life. I learned a lot from Koorosh even though he was my younger brother. Koorosh passed away on Sep. 6, 2015, however what I learned from him has been imperative of how I proceed in my career, as well as my personal life. Koorosh was a very talented young attorney, and he helped me build my practice from the ground up. His vision for my firm is still alive, and we are implementing his vision each day. I am the man that I am today because of the lessons I learned in my life from Koorosh. Thank you Koorosh, and I hope I am making you proud, because that is my goal each day.

DISCLAIMER

This publication is intended to be used for educational purposes only. No legal advice is being given, and no attorney-client relationship is intended to be created by reading this material. The author assumes no liability for any errors or omissions or for how this book or its contents are used or interpreted or for any consequences resulting directly or indirectly from the use of this book. For legal or any other advice, please consult an experienced attorney or the appropriate expert who is aware of the specific facts of your case and is knowledgeable of the law in your jurisdiction.

Khashayar Law Group
www.mysdlawyers.com
12636 High Bluff Dr.
Suite 400
San Diego CA 92130
(858) 509-1550

TESTIMONIALS

"Well, what do you say about an attorney... they are the one person you love when you need them but hate that you need them in this litigious world. I have known Daryoosh for several years now and hired him to represent me. He approaches every situation with an open mind, calm and collected demeanor and wise insight. He is always three steps ahead of everyone and obviously in three or more tangents at the same time. He has a passion for what he does and you can see when you listen to him that he truly cares about what you are going through and will help you with everything he has. He is a good man! He is a great attorney! I recommend him without reservation and know he will do good in everything he attempts to take on. I am grateful I know him."

- Jim S Burlew

****

"I have had honor to know Mr. Daryoosh Khashayar through a business matter. He demonstrated utmost skill of professionalism, trustworthy, reliability and his knowledge in this matter. He can be a source of inspiration and hope for Iranian and American community as well. I should say with confidence that he is a new phenomenon in law business."

- Iraj Saba

****

"Mr. Khashayar is a professional when it comes to law related matters. I have had the pleasure of working with him at the litigation stage and found him to be very dedicated to the well-being of clients."

- Kambiz Adibzadeh

****

TABLE OF CONTENTS

About The Author

Daryoosh Khashayar brings a unique perspective and extensive experience in the courtroom. He has knowledge in a variety of practice areas, including Commercial and Residential Real Estate, Breach of Contract, Personal Injury, Multiple Party Litigation, Malpractice, Corporations and Partnership Issues, as well as multiple Appellate Court victories. He has successfully had and completed many jury trials, as well as bench trials, and has successfully argued before the Appellate Court to reverse multiple Superior Court rulings. His unique mastery of legal concepts and ability to analyze complex issues is garnered from over 13 years of experience, and hundreds of cases. He has effectively handled countless civil & criminal cases, and has argued successfully to benefit his clients, in Superior Courts, Federal Court, as well as Court of Appeals.

Mr. Khashayar has represented and successfully litigated breach of contract, as well as tort claims, against big corporations and insurance companies, including Century 21, KB Homes, Wal-Mart, First American Title Co., Progressive, Lloyds of London, Costco, and other large insurance companies. Furthermore, he has effectively represented major lenders, brokers, mortgage companies, and local small to medium-sized businesses in California. Mr. Khashayar has won multiple awards, and received a record-breaking jury verdict of $61,587,000.00 in 2016.

Mr. Khashayar is an aggressive and creative litigator, with a steadfast focus on achieving his clients' goals. Although experienced in representing large companies, he also assists small to medium businesses, Corporations, as well as individuals. He represents his clients in complex business transactional and litigation issues, as well as related insurance coverage, and liabilities issues.

Mr. Khashayar provides years of complex litigation experience, and trial & appeal practice. He is a trial lawyer who represents plaintiffs and defendants in business, real property, and Corporate, Partnership and any Business litigations. He has obtained favorable results in all types of civil & criminal cases, some of which include Partnerships, Real Estate, Trade Secrets, Unfair Business Practices, Fraud, Breach of Contract, and Corporate issues.

Mr. Khashayar considers it his ethical duty to zealously represent his clients through the highest quality of service. He has concluded hundreds of cases, and has recovered millions of dollars for his clients, through or via settlements, judgments, awards, and verdicts, as well as multiple victories in front of the Appellate Court of California, obtaining major reversals for his clients. He has also obtained numerous defense verdicts, and favorable defense settlements for defendant clients such as a case where his client was being sued for $20 million, and settled it for only $12,000.00.

Mr. Khashayar has received the largest jury verdict on a single case (non-class action) in San Diego ($61,587,000.00), and has received multiple judgments and settlements. Some of those cases are a $1.25 million settlement on a title insurance fraud case; $750,000.00 Settlement for Insurance Fraud Claim; $648,000.00 Judgment on a Breach of contract and Fraud Case; $178,000.00 Jury Verdict on a Business Fraud and Breach of Contract case; and $205,000.00 Jury Verdict on a simple rear-end collision with little medical bills. If you are looking for an aggressive, smart and talented attorney Mr. Khashayar is your man.

About Khashayar Law Group

Our firm specializes in civil litigation, and that includes anything from personal injury to real estate business transactions, insurance bad faith, or anything in regards to civil litigation. Generally, we are hired to take a case that has already initiated by other firms about 3 to 6 months before a trial is set. While other attorneys or law firms have been working on the case, it has yet to be settled or the case is going to trial. We are retained and begin work and preparation for trial.

Components That Constitute A Viable Civil Litigation Case

In any civil litigation case, you need to first look at what the liabilities are. Is the defendant liable? You look at the evidence and ensure there is liability, and that you can connect it to the right people, who are the defendants. Once there is liability, then you must see if there are damages. Have the plaintiffs suffered any damages? If so, what are they? In a business case you look at what kind of loss—loss of future income, past income, or loss of investment. You have to see what the person lost to see if there are damages, and then move on to causation. Then you need to understand if there is liability there, and if someone is liable. There are damages, but was the person's action the cause of the damages? That is always the hardest part.

You must bring experts—economic experts, potential business experts; in a personal injury case you hire medical experts to testify that the injury and the damage that happened to the plaintiff, as well as the loss of money or the loss of business, are a direct result of the defendant's conduct or action. That is the link. Once you've established that, and see that there is liability, damages, a link between them, and have strong enough evidence to support it, then that is a good civil case to take. There is no 2 + 2 is 4. No matter how many experts you may have on your side, the other side will also have experts that they'll pay who will testify and say there is no causal effect, or damages, or that the person is not liable. They will contest all of it. It is in the experience of knowing what you have that a jury will believe, and understanding as to what the liabilities and damages are. That's how you evaluate a case when moving forward.

CHAPTER 1

TAKING THE CASE

Most cases are won or lost at the time you take the case. I learned this early on in my career. At the beginning, when you start your own firm, you will take any case that you can. You cannot be picky, however, when you have established yourself and feel comfortable about your caseload, you can be pickier. So I say when you have the time to look into each case, you take in more detail before you take them.

Don't believe everything your client tells you. I've had many potential and current clients tell me "I have an easy case" or "I have a great case." There is no such thing as an easy case, and there is no such thing as a great case. There are cases that can be proven with less effort than others, but you still need to prove all of the elements.

So, when taking a case, I first look at the facts about liability, how can I prove liability, if the case is complicated (fraud or misrepresentation), I take the jury instructions and go through the elements with the client, and see what evidence the client has to prove each element. Once I feel comfortable about taking the case on a liability issue, I need to take a good look at the client and see how I feel about presenting him/her to the jury. This might not be something you think about, but it is very important to your case. How presentable is your client to the jury? Especially when you are taking a personal injury case. The jury has to first like your client, then they have to believe that they are hurt. If they don't like your client, you can prove all you want that the other side hurt them, but when it comes to damages, the jury is not going to give your client the damages you seek.

So, evaluate the likability of your client, this is a personal thing that you will need to perfect. Will 12 random people like your client? Some things to look at follow.

- Is your client too good looking? Jury's don't tend to like people who are too good looking.
- Is your client wealthy? Jury's tend to not like people who are too wealthy.
- Is your client too robotic, which most business people are?
- Is your client too emotional?

You need to evaluate your potential clients' likability and see if you think you can help him/her to become more likable, or if they are not sympathetic.

You should do this and know the value of your case, before you are retained. This will help the entire case process.

Finally, once you are retained, you should move forward with the intent to take the case to trial. Do not take a case thinking "I am going to settle the case." Start preparing for the case to go to trial from the beginning, start looking at the jury instructions, and setting up your discovery all based on the facts that you need to prove in trial. Look at every evidence as, "how am I going to get this in to evidence" or "how can I exclude this evidence from being introduced into evidence."

When you are preparing your discovery questions, when you are preparing your deposition questions, you should do it all with the mindset of getting ready for trial. There should be a reason for each question. You only have limited time to take depositions so use the time wisely, take your time and prepare your questions. Ensure you have a goal for each witness you are deposing, you have your goal of what you are trying to get in the depo written down, and focus on those goals.

Once you have completed your depositions, you need to go over the transcripts of these and confirm you can use the testimony at trial.

Set up your discovery by proving each element of the case in mind. Review each element and ask what they have or may have regarding that particular piece of evidence. Make sure you look under each and every rock. Defendants tend to hide the ball if you let them. Reaffirm your requests are detailed and leave no room for wiggling around the responses.

When preparing your client for his/her deposition make certain you go over the details of how things are going to be asked a few times. I like to tell my clients' there are 5 responses to every question:

1. **"Yes"**
2. **"No"**
3. **"I don't know"**
4. **"I don't remember"**
5. **Most important "5 words or less"**

Let them know that it is ok not to remember a specific date or fact, as long as they generally remember the events, they do not need to worry about every single detail. This is a problem I see a lot, where my clients get nervous and try to say that they remember things that they clearly don't. You need to prepare them to be honest, and only say what they remember, they should not guess or embellish. Just listen to the question, and answer ONLY the question, nothing more, nothing less. If they take two seconds between the question and their response, this usually gives them the time to think about the question, and it will give you the time to object, if needed.

Practice this with them a few times, before their depositions. Have them tell you how the injuries have affected their life, and how they used to do things before and how they do them now, but differently. Have them go through the entire process with you, and this will make them feel more comfortable for their deposition.

CHAPTER 2

MOTION IN LIMINE

When we originally take a case, the first thing we look at is all the evidence. We put together all the evidence that we have in our favor, that we want to present to the court and the jury to build our case. More importantly all the evidence that is against us (bad for our case). Evidence is like bricks when building a house. You need them to build a house. We need every single piece of evidence to work. When we go through the evidence, first we look at each piece separately and how we are going to get them admitted into evidence. We need to evaluate each evidence individually in order to see how Civil procedure allows us to bring evidence with certain rules, and certain ways of getting evidence in. We verify what the basis is, how we are going to present it to the jury, and how we are going to get it into evidence for a judge to say, "yes, you are allowed to present this." This is our first step.

The next step is to look at the other side's evidence, and go through each piece to determine which hurt us the most, which ones we agree with, which ones we want to stipulate to bring into evidence, and which ones we potentially exclude from being presented to the jury. Those are the ones that we have potential for our Motions in Limine. A Motion in Limine is a motion that we bring into court to limit the evidence that is presented to the jury. For example, if there is a document that we believe has something that might potentially hurt our case, we might bring in a Motion in Limine to exclude it, from being presented to the jury. One reason might be that it's hearsay. Hearsay is an evidentiary statement to bring into evidence, where we say the document is an out of court statement, and it is being offered where the truth of the matter is asserted. The law says you cannot bring that in without someone coming to court and testifying to it.

There are multiple reasons why you can exclude evidence, so we review and analyze all of the defendant's and opposition's evidence. We evaluate which ones we want to exclude, and if there are any legal bases to exclude them. If we believe that there are—no matter how many, because there is no limit to how many you can file—then we file the Motions in Limine, and we make the legal argument where we present it to a judge, and the judge decides which evidence will be submitted and which evidence is excluded.

Challenges In Getting Evidence Dismissed

The general rule when you are presenting to a judge is that you don't want the judge to think that you are only trying to exclude evidence because it's bad for your case. Most judges want to present the majority of the evidence to the jury and let them decide. You have to have the legal authority, and you have to do your legal research to make sure there is legal support for your argument. When you are presenting it to the judge, you are not presenting it as "Your Honor, this is bad for my case so I don't want it in." You have to present it in the way of, "Your Honor, this is hearsay and it's against evidentiary rules for the defense to present it this way, so therefore, we need to eliminate it." Another example would be if there is evidence of prior negotiations or settlement offers, and those are strictly prohibited from being brought in to court. These are the ones where we definitely put in a Motion in Limine, because some attorneys do slip those in. They try to bring in potential offers to settle from either side, in order to win some points with the jury. Those are some of the Motions in Limine that we put in prior, so therefore, none of that happens before a jury.

How To Avoid A Motion In Limine

What you want to do when evaluating your Motions in Limine is to evaluate your credibility. If you frivolously file Motions in Limine, and you file so many of them just for the sake of filing them to potentially win one or two, you are going to start losing your credibility with that judge. You don't want to do that. You want to make certain that there is actual legal rights and authority supporting your arguments of why it should be excluded, and not because you don't want that information in front of a jury because it hurts your case. Therefore, spend time on your Motions in Limine, to confirm and verify that you have supporting legal authority for each one.

Generally speaking, I don't have more than 4 or 5, unless it's a really complicated case with a heavy set of documents. Some attorneys and people on the other side often file 15 to 20 Motions in Limine, but the adverse effect is you might be losing credibility with the judge. Once they do that, the judge reads the Motions in Limine, and after reading 4 or 5, they see that they have no merit, and the chance of the judge reading the rest in detail become slimmer. You don't want to lose that credibility.

I had a case where opposing counsel had over 20 Motions in Limine, and our side had 3. It took us a tremendous amount of time to oppose each and every one of those, which was the plan from the other side. Since I was a solo practitioner, I did not have the man power to get those responses done within the 5 days allowed for response and prepare for the trial. So, I made a strategic decision (I am not saying to do this for every case) to strongly oppose the main ones that I thought had teeth (about 5 of them). And oppose the rest in theory, with mere arguments and not getting into the details of each case sited. I did this, because I thought my time was better spent going over depositions and getting witnesses prepared and getting ready for trial, than going over these frivolous motions.

When it came to the hearing for the motions, the judge after introductions, said, let's go over these 20 plus

Motions in Limine and see why Defense counsel thought they were needed in this type of a case. He looked at defense counsel and said, please don't waist the courts' time with motions that have no merit. He said "Are you sure you want us to go over all of these, or do you want to withdraw a few that don't seem to be valid." Defense counsel looks at me and says, "Your honor in order to save the court time, we are going to withdraw a few of these, if I may have 5 minutes to review." After a few minutes he withdrew 8 of the motions and we only had to go over about 12. He had down what he wanted to do, which was to occupy me with motions instead of getting ready for trial, and I had done my best to not waste too much time on the oppositions. So the moral of the story is that, don't do these motions just to do them, do it right and the judge will evaluate them. And if the other side tries to bury you in paper, if you can have someone else respond to them do it. If not, you need to pick your battles and not waste too much time on a motion that will most likely get denied, and instead get ready for your direct or cross of witnesses.

CHAPTER 3

LEGAL INSTRUCTIONS GIVEN BY A JUDGE TO A JURY IN CIVIL CASES (JURY INSTRUCTIONS)

The jurors have to look at the jury instructions as the law provided, because it is the law that they need to follow. The jury is provided the law, but before they are provided with it, both sides or both attorneys plus the judge meet to go through them, and word them in a way that everyone agrees with. This is where the work needs to be done before going to court. This is where the instructions to the jury are the law, for whatever the causes of action that you have. For example, you have a breach of contract and negligence, and let's say in addition to that you have a fraud cause of action. You have three causes of action—negligence, breach of contract, and fraud. You need to do your research on what the California law is on giving jury instructions on those specific causes of action. California law provides you with specific instructions on every element of every single cause of action. For example, on the breach of contract, you pull up the rules, and it will tell you what the instructions are for the jury, and what the elements are that you have to prove to them.

Once you pull that up, the way that the law is drafted is there are a lot of highlighted bracket areas where, as the attorneys, we get to argue them with the other side and the judge, and we get to negotiate how it is actually presented to the jury. That's where you have to pull all of those out. As lawyers, we tend to use bigger words and try to make things a little more complicated, but when you want to give these instructions to a jury, you want to make sure that they understand it. Many of the battles between the attorneys at this stage is the use of bigger language, and making things more complicated. Others like myself want to make it easy for the jury to understand by using smaller words, lesser words, and not making it too long, or complicated. They are not going to really understand it, so we try to approve the instructions in a way that we believe the jury understands.

The way that it works is if the two sides agree on the way that it's supposed to be phrased, you inform the judge, and the judge signs off on it, and that's it. However, if there are disagreements between the parties, which is the case with regard to how to present it to the jury, that's when we present both recommendations to the judge and each make oral arguments. This is all without the jury present, even before the jury is selected. We make oral arguments in front of a judge, and the judge decides for one side's version or the other side's version, or the judge might come up with their own way of wording it, in the way they feel is best to instruct the jury on the law. There is a lot of maneuvering before it's even presented to the jury, and this is very important. Many lawyers don't focus on these jury instructions, and I think those are crucial, because that's the law that the judge presents to the jury, and they take that as 100% correct, so it's a good idea to take your time and make sure they understand it.

The more time spent on making sure that the wording is in a way where it's easy to understand, you can manipulate it in a way to where you word something so that it benefits you and your case. I personally like to use these jury instructions as the law in my closing arguments as well, which can also be helpful. Because of this, it's very important how they are drafted, and how easily it's understood.

Verdict Forms: The same goes with Verdict Forms. These are going to be the final forms the jury will see and fill out in order to get your verdict. You want them to be as easy as possible. I have seen these done, where even I did not understand what they meant. You need to make sure they are clear so there is no confusion when the jury is filling them out.

Take your time and when you are preparing the Verdict Forms, go over them with a few lay people you know. Because we as lawyers think we are being clear, but to the lay person we might not be presenting it as clear as possible. I like to take it to a few people with no legal background and make sure they understand it, and confirm that it's ok to give to the court. Don't explain it to them, have them read it, and have them tell you what it means. If they are wrong, go over it again and make sure that it's clear for non-attorneys to understand them, because at the end that is who you are writing them for.

CHAPTER 4

JURY SELECTION (ELIMINATION)

Jury selection, or jury elimination as I like to call it, because we are not actually selecting a jury, we are eliminating them. We are not picking a jury like the couple of people that we want. In California State Court, we get 6 people that we can eliminate for no reason (peremptory challenges), and we don't have to give a cause. However, we get unlimited eliminations for cause. That means for example, if my client is African American, and one of the jury members says "I hate blacks," I don't have to use one of my peremptory challenges for that juror. We tell the judge "Your Honor, this is for cause." It means that the juror cannot be fair to my client because of something that has nothing to do with the case, so therefore that juror will be eliminated without me using one of my peremptory challenges.

The peremptory challenges are, with absolutely no reason stated, I can just say, "I'd like to excuse Juror 5." That Juror 5 is gone, another one randomly takes his place, and there is no reason given for it. However, you only get 6 of those. When we are doing the jury elimination for the selection, I like to talk as little as possible. For a lot of lawyers, I think the mistake is they generally like to speak. They get up there and they talk most of the time. I think the more the jury members are talking, and the more you are listening as a lawyer, a better job you are doing on the jury selection/elimination. The reason is that in this portion of the trial, your job is to learn as much as you can about the jury members. This is probably the most important part of a jury trial, because if you are selecting jury members that are ultimately going to decide the outcome of your case, and you don't spend the majority of your time prepping for that, it's a huge mistake. You need to sit back and listen to them, do not try to convince them of your point of view, just listen to them, and learn from them. The more they are talking the better chance you have of evaluating them, and determining if they are the right jury members for your case.

Before we even get to jury selection date, I like to sit down and go through my case, and see what kind of case I want, what kind of case I am going to present, and generally what kind of a jury member am I looking for in this particular case. Every case is different. For example, if I have a business litigation case where my client is a corporation and the defendant is a corporation, and they got into a contract and now one party has breached it, and we are suing as a result of breach of contract, I'm not looking for the same kind of juror as I am when it's a personal injury case where my client has lost a limb. Those are different kinds of people that you are looking for in different kinds of cases. On the business litigation case, if I am a plaintiff suing, I'd probably want people with business backgrounds who understand the concept of oral contracts versus written contracts, people that have backgrounds in or are educated in business, or maybe people that are good with numbers.

However, if I am on a personal injury case, that has nothing to do with numbers and business, if I am a plaintiff, I'm looking for people that are in a group who are sympathetic to what my client has gone through. I would look for someone like a nurse, a school teacher, or people who, through their actions, have shown that they care about other people in their time of need. That might be the kind of people I am looking for. Now that's just a generalization, there could be nurses that are not good jurors, and there could be businessmen that are not good jurors. That's just a general search I do before we even speak to them.

Generally speaking, on a personal injury case, engineers are not going to be the best jurors for the plaintiff, because they are so technical. They look at things so that they have to be precise and reduced to a number, whereas in a personal injury case, you need to look at someone that is more general, or more open to the idea of pain and suffering, and putting some sort of a number on it. An engineer is not used to doing that, because what they do every day is very calculated. This is all general, before I even talk to them. Once we start the process, I start asking them questions about their lives and how they feel about certain things.

One of the biggest mistakes that I see attorneys make in jury selection is they try to convince the jurors of their points of view during selection. I think you lose credibility when you do that. Never argue with them, and never tell them how to think or how to feel, or tell them that this is the right way, you are right or you are wrong, even if they say something that is completely against your case.

That's actually a good thing. If a jury member says something that is completely against what you want in your case, don't shut them down, or argue with them. At that point, for example if I am standing in front of a juror in the well and I'm talking to them, I ask, "do you believe that all personal injury cases are frivolous?" If someone raises his or her hand and says, "Yes, there are too many lawsuits. They are all frivolous and they are just bringing up our insurance costs." As a plaintiff's attorney, I don't want my jury to think that all plaintiff lawyers are filing frivolous cases, or all plaintiffs themselves are being frivolous. If someone does that I always respect the juror and say, "Thank you for your statements. I know it's hard to talk in public and I appreciate your honesty." The follow up question is "does anyone here disagree with this juror?" I always try to remember the juror's name when I'm talking to them, instead of saying Juror 1 or Juror 2, call them by name, "Mr. or Ms. Smith".

I call them out. I have their names written down, and I call them Mrs. Smith, Mr. Thompson, Mrs. Taylor, whatever their names are. I try to use their names. You will make a much better connection and they will seem more like people versus just numbers. So, I say, "Mrs. Smith, thank you so much for sharing. I appreciate it. Does anyone here disagree with Mrs. Smith?" If they make those kinds of statements that are so blatant, there will be other jurors who come to your rescue, they'll make the argument for you. You do not need to do that at all, you just sit back and let them do the talking. Mr. Taylor will get up and say, "Well not all of them, there are some that are frivolous and some that are not," and let him explain how her statement that 'all plaintiffs are liars and that they exaggerate' is wrong. That alone right there—even if that original juror is selected, that juror is not going to have the credibility in the jury room, if that's the way that they are going to go. That juror is not going to have credibility when they say all plaintiffs are like this or all people are like that. So your job is to get them to talk, you want them to show their points of view, the quiet ones are the most dangerous. Make sure you get them all to say something. You don't want to sit down and not know anything about prospective members.

I don't worry about people making blatant statements that are completely against the way that we are trying to present the case. Start talking to the jury about the things they like to do. That will give you a lot of information about these people, better than the other regular questions. Can you be fair? Can you listen to the judge, and follow the law and follow the rules? Those are basic questions that don't really mean anything. Of course, the jury is going to tell you that they are going to follow the law and follow the rules, but what you want as a plaintiff's attorney is to find out if you are going to get a fair shot. Another thing that I like to do is some people or some lawyers cite from the bad parts of their case, and they try not to present. I say it from the get go. I say it from the beginning and let them know that information. The jurors are very smart people, they will understand.

For example, if you have a personal injury case and your client misses 6 months of treatment before she starts going to the doctor. There is a 6-month gap, and the defense is going to bring that up. There is no reason not to bring it up and talk about it in jury selection, because that's going to be something that they discuss in the jury room later. I always bring that up and tell them, talk to them about it. You can just say, "Anyone please raise your hand if you think if someone has back pain they have to immediately go to the doctor, and if they wait a few months, you don't believe that they are hurt." A few might raise their hands, and few might not. Then you get their limits as to the time. Get them to talk about their beliefs. "What is the limit where you think a person should wait and after that it's not proper?", and then let them talk. Let them bring it up and some people might say two months, some people might say four months, and you let them talk amongst each other, get as many of them to talk as possible. You just want them to see there are more reasons for people to wait, and the time varies from person to person, so when the defense doctor gets on the stand and says anything more than 4 weeks is not reasonable, you know many of them have said much more.

One juror says two months, and another juror says nine months. The nine-month juror says, "Look, two months is simply not enough. I've had back pain, I didn't go for six months because my work wouldn't let me." That logic goes out to the rest of the jurors. They are talking amongst themselves, and all you are doing is throwing things out there and letting them talk. Another thing that I like to do, besides the bad part that I don't want to hide and I want to put it out there, whatever you think of as an attorney or portions of the case that you don't even like a little bit, which could potentially hurt your case, this is the time to bring it up. If you don't, they'll come up in evidence and what will happen is the jury will wonder why you were hiding it from them. You are going to lose credibility. Bring it up during your opening, bring it up as much as you can, and let them know.

Another issue I always bring up in regards to a civil case is the fact that it's by preponderance of the evidence, versus a criminal case, which is beyond all reasonable doubt. Everyone knows beyond all reasonable doubt from criminal movies, and some people might have served on criminal juries. You want to make sure that they understand the difference. As the plaintiff's lawyer, you do not have to prove beyond a reasonable doubt that you were hurt, that you suffered damages, that the contract was breached, or in a business litigation matter, that the other side owes you money. That doesn't have to be beyond a reasonable doubt, it must be on what is called a preponderance of the evidence. I always like to show the jury a little scale with my hands, all that means is 50.001%.

If I can show you that my side is "likely" true, you must, by the law come back with a verdict in my favor. A lot of people don't like that. Many people wonder if they're not sure, why do they have to do that? You want them to talk about it, because you want those people to speak out. Then others will come up, you ask them the same question, and you say what it is and why you need to follow the law, if the law tells you one way or another. I've had judges interrupt here at times, and tell them that the law and the instructions they are going to get will ask if they can follow it. Now, when the judge agrees with you as an attorney, that gives you another measure of credibility with the jury.

I've had a few instances where judges actually interrupt and tell the jurors, Mr. Khashayar is correct. That's the law, and even if you don't feel comfortable, you must abide by the law. Can you do that? They all say yes. The question is not whether they say yes or no. It's the authority, especially now that a judge has given them. "Hey, even though I don't agree with some of the law, if the judge instructs me, I will follow it," and other people will say it, too. The one or two jury members that might say, "no I won't," once again, I'm not worried about them, because they've lost credibility. They just told an entire jury room that even if the law says one thing, they won't abide by it. That's not an issue. Don't worry about what they say. Just make sure that it's talked about.

Another major issue to bring up during jury selection is the amount of damages. First of all, a lot of people might have a moral issue, or just some sort of conflict, with giving money to someone for either pain and suffering, or breach of contract, or any kind of business litigation. They just don't like that. You ask them about it. Does anyone here have any issues with that? Does anyone think there is too much money being awarded in lawsuits? I'm sure that people are going to raise their hands. We've all heard the McDonald's case, and people are going to say $7 million for a cup of coffee is ridiculous. I've heard this a hundred times from jury members, and they all know that. You want them to talk about that. You want them to bring those subjects up.

"Raise your hands if you think that no matter what the evidence shows, that you will in your head have a cap that I cannot give over more than $100,000 or a million dollars for a personal injury case, or any kind of a case." Some people will raise their hands, and some people will bring up the subject that I think that a million dollars for any kind of personal injury is just too much. Then you explain it to them. Okay, what if the person were missing two legs? It's still too much. What if the person has a brain injury and couldn't function? So, you go through a couple of analyses, and if they still say that, then it's actually a good thing because now they seem unreasonable to the rest of the jury members. Some other jury member will come to your rescue. They will come and say "Of course, $100,000 might be enough for someone who says my back hurts, but if the person has a brain injury and has to be fed through the rest of their lives, $100,000 is nowhere near enough." They'll come to your rescue.

Then whatever you think the value of your case is, for example, if I have a business litigation case and my client lost a million dollars in deals, then potentially, in the future, my experts are going to testify that you would have lost $6 million to $8 million. I know in my head that my client's damages are somewhere between $7 million to $9 million dollars. I want to make sure that this jury is ready and prepared with those sorts of numbers. So, I ask that what if we prove to you, with the preponderance of the evidence, that my client was injured, or the other side had breached an agreement or for whatever reason, that they are entitled to $15 million. Does anyone here have a problem with that number? If someone says something I thank them. Always thank people when they make a response.

It's very hard to open up and say what you think in front of a big group of people, and people are very reluctant to do that any time. No matter good, bad, or different, however you feel about the statement made by any jury members, you want to thank them, because everyone else in that room is watching you. If you don't thank them and give them respect, then they are not going to give you credibility, and they are not going to feel comfortable raising their hands to talk to you, and they might say something that will benefit you in one way or another. You want to make sure that you always thank them. When you thank them, they'll come back and they'll talk to you more. Whatever amount that I believe I'm going to be asking for at the end of a case, I start talking numbers at least one and a half to two times that in jury selection.

I want the jurors to be comfortable with the idea of that kind of money from the beginning. It's the first thing I mention to them, and I'm not even talking about this case. They have no idea that I'm only going to ask for $8 million, because I'm in front of them talking as if, for example, if a case is proven to you that a person is damaged and justifiably, by preponderance of the evidence, they are entitled to $20 million, who here would feel uncomfortable doing that? Who here would feel comfortable with that? You make them raise their hands, so they would be comfortable. You should call them out and make them respond. It doesn't necessarily make it so that it's what is going to happen, but you're putting those numbers out there.

It's very beneficial to do that from the start. Then when you go to the end, and you are asking for $8 million to $9 million, they've already been conditioned with a number in their head. They are already thinking this attorney is going to ask for between $15 million to $20 million. When you are asking for $8.5 million, you are not that greedy as asking for what you did. However, they've been predisposed to big enough numbers. That is very crucial when you are speaking about the damages, is talk about the numbers and make sure they do a lot of the talking. As I said at the beginning, it's very crucial that you sit back and let them talk. This is also all going to depend on how a judge presiding in your case evaluates the timeframe. I've had judges give me 30 minutes, 45 minutes, and the most has been an hour. I've never had any judge let me talk for more than an hour. That was a case that went on for about a month and a half. We needed 15 or 18 jury members, and there were a lot of alternatives.

You need to get the jury members to talk and do not interrupt them. I've seen a lot of times where opposing counsel starts interrupting one juror and moves on to another juror. You lose credibility doing that. Another issue with regards to jury selection is to always confirm your clients are available to attend. I had a case where the defense counsel did not bring their client to jury selection. He thought it was not important. He actually stood and asked the jury members, "Do you think it's a big deal that my client is not here? He had other things to do." They spoke up against him, and responded with, "we all have other things to do, why are we here and he is not?" He ended up using most of his peremptory challenges on those jurors and some of them were actually in his favor, but he had angered them that much by his client not showing up.

Always confirm your clients are available to attend trial from the beginning. They do not have to be there during jury selection, but ensure that they are and throughout the whole trial each and every day. If they are missing for even one day, there has to be a good reason, and you should tell the judge in advance to let the jury know, because they all have better places to be as well. They have work, they have families, they have other things, and it's disrespectful to them if one of the parties say, "I'm not going to show up today." They don't have to be there by law, but you should ensure, as a litigation attorney, that you have your client(s) available to attend and ready to go every single day.

Once we select a jury, then the judge swears the jury in. Once they are sworn in, depending on what time of the day it is, there might be a lunch break or afternoon break. Then the judge reads the jury the jury instructions that we had previously agreed to and written out, and now that they've had the instructions and the law, then the opening statements begin, depending on what time of the day it is. If it is the end of the day, they can come back tomorrow morning for the opening statements, or after lunch, then you start your trial with opening statements from each side.

CHAPTER 5

OPENING STATEMENTS

Opening statements are the outline of a case that you are presenting to the jury. What you usually want to do before the opening statement is to come up with a theme for your case. A theme that you are going to go through, and show to a jury how your case will be presented. For example, we had a legal malpractice case where our client's attorney, who was an attorney for over 30 years, at the end of his career was letting his staff just handle most of the legal work. Some of the work fell through the cracks, and our client ended up losing a significant amount of money as a result of this attorney not being there, and not looking over all the documents that were being presented through the firm. Our theme for that case was "a ship without a captain."

That's how we presented it from the opening. I presented it to them as a law firm being run without an attorney looking over everything, is like a ship being out in the ocean without its captain. It's going, it's moving, we just don't know where or how it's going to end up.

Come up with a theme, something they will connect with or an analogy that you can come back to. After the opening, hint at it throughout your analysis of the whole case, and it should be a part of your closing. Opening statements are very important, because it's where you tell the jury your story. You put it in a timeline. The reason why a timeline is important in an opening statement is because while you are in a jury trial, witnesses don't always show up in the chronological order that you want. You are going to have to take witnesses out of order.

You are going to have opposing side's witnesses testify during your time, and yours testifying through their time. It's just the reality of a trial. The timeline is important, because if for example, you have a business litigation case, you might have an expert on your damages showing up on the 3rd day of trial, before you even establish liability. They are not going to say who that person is or why they are talking about that, unless you've broken it down in the timeline who, what, where, and how you are going to get there. You explain that to them in that opening. Give them the roadmap to where you think the case is going to go. Given the timeline of the events that happened with the parties that were involved, go through the analysis. This is not the place to argue your case. Don't try to convince them that your case is right, or your rights are being violated, and you are in the right and the defense is in the wrong.

This is not the time to do that, and you are going to lose credibility by doing that, if there are objections by the other side or the judge. Always start by saying the evidence will show, and go through what you believe that the evidence will show. That's not an argument, that's just stating the facts, saying what you think the evidence will show. Make the opening short. You don't need to go through a lot of argument, just enough that you give them the information, so that they know where the case is going, what your position is, and why you believe you are entitled to be there and to take their time.

Another thing to remember is under promise and over deliver, one of my dear friends, Robert Hamparyan, who is an excellent trial lawyer always told me to do this, and it's great advice. What does that mean? Don't set up an opening and promise them all this evidence that is going to come in, and that all these people are going to say X, Y and Z, if you are not 100% sure it is going to happen. If you do and you, for example, say "You are going to see a document that shows my client did this and the defendant did this," but for some reason, that document might not come into evidence. Unless you have stipulated with opposing counsel that the evidence is going to come in, don't make that promise. There might be some motion from the other side halfway through the trial, or a witness that was supposed to authenticate that document doesn't show up, there is a family emergency, or something is going to happen. That's just normal life. Now that you've stated that the document is going to show X, Y, or Z in opening, and then it ends up not coming in and that document doesn't show X, Y, or Z, now you've lost credibility, because the jury is taking notes of everything you do. Everything you say at the beginning, there are good jury members taking notes, and they are going to go back in the jury room and they are going to say "Remember in opening, Mr. Khashayar promised us he was going to bring this document? That never happened." Now I've lost credibility with that juror, and he brings it up and the others go, "Yeah. He did say that. Where was that document? Maybe he was trying to convince us of things that are not true."

Now, I've lost credibility and the jury is going to make their decisions based on something that might not have to do with anything, but I created that by making a promise that I couldn't deliver on. Always under promise and over deliver. Just go through the analysis of what the case is, and the timeline of what happened. You don't need to make arguments, or talk about the evidence, unless you are 100% sure it's being submitted, and there is a stipulation previously by the other side about this piece of evidence. Then you can talk about it, but always remember to under promise and over deliver. Following, make your opening—it doesn't have to be too long and you don't have to make any arguments, just make sure you set a road map to your story. Make sure it's simple and to the point. The way you tell a story matters, the order you tell a story matters. For example, you have a client who was driving and another party ran a red light and hit him and he is injured as a result. You could start by telling the jury that he woke up that morning as he did every other day, and he took a different route to go to work that morning, and as he was going through the green light he was hit by the defendant. This is accurate, however by going through it to tell the jury this part first you are predisposing them of forming some sort of negative opinion about your client before you have even mentioned the defendant. For instance, the jury members could think, well he should have taken a different route. It is typical to blame the victim so don't give them the opportunity.

Instead start the story by telling the jury from the defendants' point of view. How the Defendant got up that morning and was in a hurry and had a bad day, and did not see the light because he was not paying attention, and he crashed into your client, Ms. Jones. Just by giving the story from the defendants' point of view first, you will have jury members already thinking that the defendant is at fault, before they even get a chance to learn what your client did. This is because we tend to blame the victims, and by telling the jury first that our client got up and took a different route because he thought it was a beautiful day, they are going to immediately think, well he could have avoided this whole thing if he had gone his normal route. They will start blaming the Plaintiff for deciding to take a different route. Keep that in mind when preparing your opening statement.

Once you finish your story and set up the theme for your case, always thank the jury for their time, on your behalf as well as on your clients' behalf. Then sit down and start taking notes while opposing counsel gives his/her opening statement. This is where you have to take good notes.

I take really good notes when the other side is presenting their opening statements, because the other side might not take my advice and make promises that they know they can't deliver, or make arguments that they might not be able to deliver on later. I take really good notes, and then after they are done with their opening statements, I actually contact the court reporter and I order a transcript of their opening statements. I will use that for my closing arguments at a later date. As to my point earlier, if through the trial, any of those promises that the counsel just made to the jury were not fulfilled, and a lot of times they are going to make promises that are not going to be proven, then I get the transcript and use that to benefit my case. I show the jury this is what was promised by opposing counsel, and it's a big zero. That's how you attack their credibility later. Once your opening is done, don't just sit down and forget about it. Sit down, take notes, and put together a list of specific promises that opposing counsel is making, and then order the transcripts and wait. I promise you at least 2 or 3 of those promises are not going to be proven, and you can make points later during the closing arguments.

CHAPTER 6

DIRECT EXAMS

Direct exam is when you are examining your own witnesses or your own client. This is actually one of the hardest parts of the case, because you are not allowed to have what's called leading questions. I can't ask my client, "Isn't it true that you performed everything in the contract and the other guy breached it?" That's just a yes or no question, which means that it's going to get objected to. I can't lead him into questions with answers that I want. I have to ask open ended questions such as, "What did you do with the defendant in regards to this building," and he has to explain, "We entered into a contract, and we did X, Y, or Z." He has to do that. The hardest part on that is to prep before going to trial. I sit down with my clients on at least 3 separate occasions, and I go through the questions and answers, because they are not used to the way they are supposed to be asked a question.

They might think you are asking one thing and go off on a tangent, when you want them to go a certain way, because we are asking open ended questions. It's usually with questions such as, "When you met the defendant, what happened next?" "I saw the defendant at this meeting and he presented an offer to enter into an agreement." "So, he presented it to you. Is that correct?" "Yes." "What was the agreement?" Then he has to explain the terms of the agreement as he understood it. We have to ask these kinds of questions. The first thing I do is I sit down with my clients, and I go through a full question and answer session. I have them take notes of where I am going with my questions, and they are going to respond with how they are going to respond during trial. Then I type it all up for them, and they go and read it a couple of times. I read it to them or I have them read it, and I read them their deposition, which is key. I make sure that they read their depositions at least once or twice before their testimony.

That's very crucial, because people forget. They forget things they stated, and they are not lying, just forgetting. You want to make sure that they lead to where they testified before. If there is any written discovery that was done previously, go through that with them. Have them read it again. Make sure that you and your client are on the same page with regards to the direct exam, and where you believe the direct exam is going to go. When you are asking the questions, you do not want the client to be thinking one thing when you are thinking another. The prep work is the most crucial part of the direct exam, and you need to ensure, as an attorney, that you are good with asking the same kind of question in multiple ways, and are ready for objections from the other side.

What I usually do is I have another attorney, usually an associate in my office or a friend and colleague, after the first time I prepare my clients, they study it and they come back a second time. The second time, I have another attorney sit there while I ask the direct questions of the client, and they will start objecting. I will have another associate or somebody pretend to be the judge, and they do overruling objections or sustaining. Most of them will be sustained, because we want to be prepared for multiple ways of asking the question. If, for example, I ask the question and they object to it as leading, I'm going to have to rephrase it. I will rephrase it in another way. Then the client understands where I am going with it, and then they will answer it again in a different way. The majority of the work to be done for the direct exam is by the client, because you are the expert who has done this before, they have not.

Make sure they are prepared for the direct examination, and make sure they know where you are going with your questions. Where you are going would mean the path of, when I say, "why was the contract breached as far as you understand it?" Then he could explain, "Well, the defendant sent me an email and said X, Y & Z," and not the reason they believe that the defendant breached the contract. You explain to them the legal bases for your case and where they should be going, and you move forward from there. This is a lot of prep work with regards to the direct exam. Most of it is prep work. It's the same thing with other witnesses. You are not going to be able to prep your neutral witnesses, your experts. You sit down and you go through it with your experts, things that you think will be asked. What you must consider when you talk to anyone else besides your client. With your client, you are preparing them for their direct exam and or preparing them for their cross exam.

Everything that you say to them, or they say to you, is attorney-client privileged, and no one could ever ask about it. However, if you have other witnesses that are going to testify, for example, an expert witness, you can't prepare an expert witness, because whatever you tell them is discoverable. The other side can ask questions like, "Hey, business expert Smith, what did Mr. Khashayar tell you in regards to this case?" and he has to answer everything I told him about this case. I can't tell him, "Hey, let's prep for your direct exam. Here are the questions I am going to ask and here is how you are going to respond." That's all on him. He actually prepares the reports as to what his opinions are, he sends it to us, and we do our direct exam based on that report.

There is no preparation for anybody else. You don't want to prepare a 3rd party or a witness that's a neutral party, because if you do that, now the other side gets to ask questions of that person regarding your communication with them, and that's definitely something you don't want to do. The only person you would prepare would be your client, and if it's a corporation it's under corporate protection with regards to being a client of yours so you prepare the corporation representative.

I have prepared many witnesses for trial, and the hardest thing to do is to be able to ask the right question, in order to have the witness know where you are going with the question. This is difficult because you are not supposed to ask leading questions, so having the witness explain what happened next is usually the best way to get them to tell their story. However, sometimes you get witnesses who get nervous when they get on the stand and say things that are not relevant to anything you are asking. So you need to take your time and start them over again, and if needed lead them to where you want to go. If the other side objects, then you can ask it again. It's ok. But at least you are giving your witness a clue as to where you are going with that question.

Getting Evidence admitted into Evidence

Prior to trial when you are preparing your direct exam of each witness, you need to allocate each piece that is going to be introduced into evidence to each witness who will be testifying as to that evidence. For example, if there is an email you want to introduce into evidence, you need to make sure you ask one of the parties who received or sent the email to authenticate the email before you can introduce it into evidence. Therefore, for each exhibit I intend to introduce into evidence, I put the name of the person who needs to testify as to getting that exhibit into evidence. So, when a witness is on the stand, I have a check list of exhibits I need to ask about from that particular witness. Make sure that you have all your exhibits lined up with a witness who can authenticate it, or somehow get it into evidence.

If you have exhibits that witnesses from the opposing side will testify to, you need to identify those exhibits and make sure you have either a deposition transcript where that witness has authenticated the exhibit, or written discovery where the witness has either authenticated the exhibit or confirmed its receipt.

Some demonstrative exhibits can be stipulated to get into evidence. For example if you want to introduce a google map view from above of a scene of an accident, you can show the opposing side the photo, or blow it up and if its accurate, they can stipulate to have you introduce it into evidence.

Make sure that you have done either one of these on each and every piece of evidence you are intending to introduce, or you might not be able to use it.

CHAPTER 7

DIRECT EXAMS OF EXPERT WITNESSES

The approach I take at direct exams of my experts is, first, all of these experts are going to have their CVs, curriculum vitae. I go through it very slowly to the jury. Have the expert tell everyone why he or she is an expert in their field. If our expert is an accountant trying to explain to the juries why there are future injuries to our clients, because they lost this business deal and what the valuation of that is, the jury has to believe that the person is credible. You go through all of their education and make sure when you are presenting this to go very slow, because you want the jury to understand why he is an expert. "You went to college, what college did you go to? Did you go to graduate school? What graduate school did you go to?"

You go through their CV, and every speech that they've given, every book that they've written. Any reason you think that he or she is an expert in that field, we ask them questions about it. "Explain it more for us.

Why did you do this? Why is it important that you have this specific certification?" Then, once you believe that they've established that they are an expert in that field, then you go through their reports. You say, "Mr. Expert Smith, what were you hired to do in this case?" They'll tell you that they were hired to evaluate a business, and to give projections for the future income of that business. Then I ask, "In doing that, what steps did you take?" Then we'll let them go through every single step.

Now, from previously asking him those questions and having gone over the report, you need to know all the steps. Being on the stand sometimes, these experts might skip a step, or forget that they went to 5 different businesses in that specific location and they'll say I went to 4 different businesses. If you have a checklist of everything that they have done, which you should have done in previous sessions with them, if they miss one, you say, "Mr. Expert Smith, isn't it true that you also went to so and so, and did X, or Y, or Z," and he will correct you and say, "Yes, I forgot I did that." Make sure that they go through and explain to the jury every step that they took before coming to their conclusions.

Then you have them explain the opinions that they have formed. We know what they are based on, but have them explain what they are and have them explain the numbers. Juries are very visual. If you can get experts to have presentations in PowerPoint, or big boards that they can show with a laser pointer, have some graphics to build credibility. It also shows that they have more knowledge and experience of showing the jury what it is in the way they talk to them. Make sure that they have PowerPoint or some kind of visual aids to show them where we came to our opinions, and how we came up with them. Then, the expert will explain to the jury why he believes in his expert opinion that the damages should be X, Y, or Z. Make sure that you have clear testimony of the standard of testimony. What that means is that if, for example, your expert is a doctor who is testifying on future damages, make sure you clarify that his testimony is "to a reasonable medical certainty" which is the standard. Make sure you understand the standard needed for each expert testimony and your final question can be "Dr. your testimony regarding X, Y, or Z, was that to a reasonable

Medical Certainty? And go through all his testimony and ensure the record is clear that he is making that testimony to a reasonable medical certainty. Once you accomplish that, then you can move on as your direct exam is complete as to that specific expert.

Direct Exams Of Neutral Witnesses

Direct exams of neutral witnesses are tricky, because you are technically allowed to talk to them before a trial, but everything you say to them is going to be asked by the other side. For example, we are back at the breach of contract case, where two people are involved in litigation with regards to a business deal that went bad. If we have a witness that has no stake in the matter, and that witness was there at the time of signing, and he knows that he witnessed the defendant telling the plaintiff, "I will give you that million dollars in 30 days, I promise, as I shake your hand." If for some reason it is relevant that we need that witness to testify, what I do in preparation, if we believe that's what happened, is I have an investigator contact them. I don't contact the witnesses myself directly, because at that point I wouldn't want to be a witness to the case and have to be called on to the stand.

We have an investigator contact them and say, "We were told that you were present at this meeting, is that true?" Once they say yes, we ask them "Can you tell us what you witnessed?" You don't want to tell them what the client is saying, and you don't want to tell them anything about your case or what your case is about. You just want them to be neutral. You want them to be honest, and tell you what they actually remember. You just ask them, "What did you witness? Were you there?" and have them type up what they think happened. Then the investigator will send that to the attorney, and I will review it for something that supports what the client said and is beneficial. Have that put in a declaration form under penalty of perjury, and then have the investigator take that to the same party and have them sign the declaration. The reason for that is sometimes people change their minds, and you need this to prove what they originally stated.

I had a client in the same type of breach of contract case where the witness was saying the same kind of things, like, "I witnessed the contract and this is what was said." However, I had actually gotten them to sign a declaration. When coming to trial, he gets on the stand and says, "No, I never said that. The person says X, Y, or Z. Anyone who says so is not telling the truth. I didn't witness anything at all. All I saw was them shaking hands and I didn't hear anything." Then what you do in that moment is present the declaration. That declaration does not have to be introduced into evidence, it does not have to be put on the exhibit list, because it's for impeachment purposes only. As an attorney you expect the witnesses that you put on the stand to tell the truth. You don't expect them to get up and lie.

Therefore, you don't need to put that declaration into evidence, unless that person gets on the stand and says something that is completely contradictory to what they told your investigator a year ago under penalty of perjury. If they do that, then you can bring it in as impeachment. You show them the declaration and you say, "Sir, isn't that your signature?" If it is their signature they usually agree and if they don't, you bring in the investigator to confirm it. Then you say, "There in that declaration, you stated that the person said I will get you the million dollars in 30 days. Now, you are telling the jury something different. Understand it was under the penalty of perjury and it was under the same oath that you just took today." You explain all of that and you call them on their lie. That's why you get the declarations right away, because in the beginning, witnesses and evidence or people are good with one another for whatever reason, but life happens and they may change their minds.

While they are telling you that is what happened and that's what I am going to say, and I am going to tell the truth, you have them sign a declaration under penalty of perjury. You most likely won't have to use it, but you have it just in case something happens and they decide for whatever reason not to be honest with the court. You don't want to be standing there with egg on your face when you expected them to say one thing, but now they are saying something else. Furthermore, with regards to neutral witnesses, most of them might have their deposition taken, which you will also have as well to use for impeachment purposes.

I have had a neutral witness who was my client's friend at the time of the contract say one thing, and get on the stand (a couple of years later), and say the complete opposite. He had forgotten that I had him sign a declaration so when I showed that to him on the stand, he claimed that he was lying when he signed the declaration and now he was telling the truth. The jury punished the defendant for that and we got a very good verdict. Always be prepared for witnesses to change their stories. Make sure you get them to sign a declaration under penalty of perjury early on in the case.

CHAPTER 8

CROSS EXAMINATION IN A TRIAL

Cross examination is one of the parts of trial that I personally enjoy the most. Even though it has much more prep work on your end versus the client's direct exam. In cross examination, you should know the answer of every question that you are asking them. First, let's go over the cross exam of a party, the defendant, or a witness or someone that is not an expert witness. I start by going through all of their depositions and transcripts of any testimony under oath. I pick out all the questions that I want in order to elicit a response that I think is favorable and appropriate for our case, and I ask it in a yes or no question. For example, in the deposition transcript, the defendant said I entered into the contract because I thought the building was worth $5 million. When I want to establish that, I ask the defendant, "Isn't it true that the reason you entered into this contract is that you thought that the building was worth $5 million?"

Next to that question I write what's called a line and page. I write the page of the deposition of where I got that statement from, and all the lines that are inclusive. For example, page 5, line 17 to 32 is where he makes that question and answer. The reason I do that on every question is because if he says on the stand, "No, that wasn't the reason," then I can bring that in as evidence with regards to his deposition. Now hopefully when you took the deposition, you did proper follow up questions, such as "is that the only reason you entered into the contract?" and if he says, yes, now you have all the reasons on the record. I would also keep following up in the deposition, "So there is no other reason, correct?" Once you have his yes to that, he can't say in trial there are other reasons, without looking like he is hiding something.

The way to bring that deposition as evidence in a trial is you ask the question, "Sir, do you recall giving a deposition on this matter?" He'll say yes. "Do you recall taking an oath when you took that deposition?" He'll say yes, I recall that. "Do you recall when you took that oath, you promised to tell the truth?" He'll say yes. "Were you telling the truth at the time you gave that deposition?" He is going to say yes, or he may say no, which would be great for us. He is going to say yes, though.

"So now that we've established that you were telling the truth under penalty of perjury at that deposition, I'm going to read for the record your deposition dated, and give the date for the record and the page and line. Then you read for the record, "Question: what was the reason you entered into this contract? Answer: I entered into this contract because I believed that the value of the building was worth $5 million." Once I read that I say, "Sir, do you recall now that it's what you said at your deposition?" "Yes." "However, you just told the jury that it's not the reason you entered it. Were you telling the truth then or are you telling the truth now?" "It's more complicated." "No, it's not. It's a simple question. Back then for the same question you said it was $5 million, now you are saying that it's not the reason. Are you lying now or were you lying then?"

Then the objections will come from the other side. That's all you need to do. You've already made your point to the jury. Unless there is any other reason, I would leave it at that point and make a comment regarding his truthfulness and move on. The way you ask questions is key, because if you don't ask it in a way that the transcript reads, it is in direct conflict with your answer, and the other side will object to you even reading it, if it's not a properly phrased question. For example, the same question with regards to the value of the building being the reason he entered into a contract. If the question in the deposition says, why did you enter into the contract? Answer: because I believed the building would be worth $5 million.

A bad way of forming a question would be "Isn't it true that you believed the value of the building to be over $5 million, and that's the only reason you entered into the contract?" The fact that you said that it was the only reason, that's not what he stated. Therefore, that's not a direct conflict, and a judge could potentially say you can't read that into evidence because he is not really contradicting that. What he testified was it was the reason, but it wasn't the only reason. You must ensure that when you are preparing your cross examination, and when you read the question out loud "Isn't it true that..." whatever statement follows that should be in direct connection with the response that the defendant is making in his deposition. That way, when you are doing it, it just flows. Isn't it true, isn't it true, and isn't it true, and you want him to say yes, yes, and yes.

Follow your path and your logic in how you are establishing the evidence, and any time that he says no, then what you do is bring that in as evidence. A lot of times what the defendants say is "no, but…" and then they go on and try to explain it. That is the perfect time to do an objection, non-responsive, and move to strike anything other than no. That is because you've asked a specific question. You asked isn't it true that X, Y, or Z? That's a yes or no question. Don't let them start explaining and continuing to why. As soon as he does that, you just object. "Objection, Your Honor. Non Responsive. Move to strike everything after the answer to the question," and the judge will move to stop it. He'll read it and he'll see that the question was a yes or no. If the question was a yes or no, and they said yes, and then go on to explain, you should strike everything after that.

A lot of people will keep doing that, and I've had judges, after I've made a few objections, actually tell the person on the stand, "Listen to the question. You are not answering it, and you are wasting time." Once a judge does that to a party on a stand, there is a complete loss of credibility, and the jury always gives credibility where the judge says. If the judge actually interrupts or does anything like that, it really is helping you and your case. It's the same thing with prepping your clients. You must make sure that they don't do anything with regards to their cross exams that might upset the judge as well. With regard to witnesses, in a cross exam, I would go through all of their depositions, I would make sure that every question I'm asking them is properly worded, and it's all in a yes or no format. The next thing to do is, if there are any documents that you need to admit into evidence, you ensure that they are properly authenticated.

For example, if a document has the defendant's signature on it, hopefully, in a deposition, you've asked them, "Is this your signature?" If they said yes, then they've already admitted to that, and when you do your cross exam, you make sure you put in the line and page of exactly where they identified in that document, and then you present it to them in trial and say, "Is this your signature?" If they say no, you can go back and do the line and page where they authenticated it before. If they say yes, then you submit it into evidence. You need to ensure that this is properly submitted into evidence, because if it is not, unless they are agreed to by both sides, the jury does not get to see those documents or any of that evidence later. You want to make sure they are properly authenticated, then submitted into evidence.

If you do have 3rd party neutral witnesses, I would definitely get all of their depositions and do the same as before. If you don't have their depositions, confirm that you have at least a declaration from them so you can do the line and page with regards to their declarations. If there are surprise witnesses that just come in at the last minute, your best path to take is to attack their credibility. If you have nothing that attacks their actual statements from before, and if it's a 3rd party and you are being sent back for trial, and for some reason the judge allows this witness to come in, then you need to establish some sort of a connection with the other side. For example, "Isn't it true that you are related to the other side?" Or "isn't it true that you've worked with defense counsel before?" or something along these lines.

If you don't see a connection with them, but they've already given a statement to the other side, I would try to ask for a short recess. Leave the courtroom and attempt to talk to that person with an investigator, and have them provide me with a statement. What happens often is that those people don't talk to you. They refuse to do it. On one case where a defendant brought in a last-minute witness, I didn't tell the judge why I needed a break. I just told him "Your Honor, I need a quick break to prep for this new witness." I went outside and saw the witness outside in the hallway. I approached that witness with my investigator, and I said I would like to talk to you for 5 minutes about what you are testifying.

At that moment, he refused, and with opposing counsel, went to another room. In that situation during my cross, I had no idea what he was going to say. Once he began, he stated that my client had confessed to him that he was wrong in the breach, and had told him all these other things. I told him during my cross exam, "Sir, you are supposed to be a neutral party, correct?" He said yes. "You just told this jury you had no stake in this matter, who wins or loses, you have absolutely no stake in it. Isn't that correct?" He said yes. I said, "Well, previous to coming here today, you spoke with opposing counsel, correct?" He said yes. I said, "In fact you were probably in his office before you came here." He said yes. I said, "You spoke with him. You went to his office, however, during breaks I came to ask you a question just to see what you were going to say and you refused to talk to me. Isn't that true?" He said yes.

"If you are trying to be neutral to both sides why did you talk to one side and not the other?" He danced around the question, but ultimately could not respond because he had talked to the other side at length and would not even talk to me for 5 minutes. The key to these cross exams is not to try to punish the witness, treat them with respect and be very nice and polite. Let the jury be the one who punishes them. If the jury sees you calling the person a liar and it looks like you are badgering them, they will not feel the need to help you and your client. There is a fine line to make your point, but do it in a manner that does not seem like you are too arrogant or pushy.

The point of that cross was to basically attack his credibility. Afterwards, when I talked to the jury, they gave his statement absolutely no weight, because he refused to talk to me, and was supposed to be a neutral witness that had nothing to gain, and who supposedly had witnessed my client confess to the breach. That would be a worst-case scenario where you have to think on your toes, when you are not prepared for a witness. Usually judges do not allow that kind of sandbagging, but you can never predict things, and if it does happen then you go with it, and think quickly to accomplish what you can and need.

CHAPTER 9

CROSS EXAMINATION OF EXPERT WITNESSES

With the expert cross exams, these people are professionals. They are either doctors or accountants, and he or she is an expert in their field. I think one of the biggest mistakes people make is try to argue the expertise, and that is definitely not the way to do it. What I do first is, I do my due diligence and research the expert. Look them up online, look up what they do for a living, look at how many times they have testified, and look at their website and how they describe themselves. Most of them are bought and paid for experts, and they have websites that say "I am an expert" and they list about 30 to 40 things that they are an expert in. You need to go back and do your research in what they do and what he or she is an expert in. For example, we had a case where it was a dental syringe issue, and the expert testified on the stand that he is an expert in all dental syringes.

We went to his website and found out that he had testified as an expert, and he listed on his website over 35 different things that he was an expert in, including agriculture, automotive, automotive speeding, vegetables, dental syringes, media, Hollywood, etc. The list went on and on of what he was an expert in. I had all of that in front of me. Furthermore, I researched with regards to how these experts usually testify on both sides of the case. It doesn't matter who pays them, they'll actually use that to their advantage when they get up on the stand to show credibility, say "I do 50/50 work. Plaintiff and defense." I use that against them, if they are the defense's experts. For example, this expert said that my client's dental syringe had no value and because of X, Y, or Z reasons he believes my client has zero damages, because this particular product had zero value.

What I did was went back and pulled up cases where he had testified as a plaintiff for medical products, and using the same reasoning that he is saying my client's case doesn't have value, he was saying because of these, it does have value. That's all they do. Experts use a format. They plug in, and it either does have value or it doesn't depending on who hired them. So, I pull his transcripts from previous testimony during my cross exam. I get up and I tell the jury, "Okay Sir, you just told this jury for over 2-and-a-half hours how you are an expert in dental syringes. Is that correct?" Yes. "You are qualified as to testify as to dental syringes. Correct?" Yes. "Is your website so and so?" They'll say yes, and I'll print out the website and I'll put up the printouts on the board. I go through all of the portions of the law where he has testified for as an expert and I go through it very slowly for the jury. "You have testified as an expert in agriculture, sir. Isn't that correct?" He'll say yes. "You have testified in the automotive industry. Isn't that correct?" Yes. "You have testified in fruit, gasoline, in airplanes, etc."

I go through all of the 35 fields, and by the time I get to the end, if you do it slow enough, the jury understands that this expert will testify for whatever you pay him. He is not really an expert. He does some research online, and gets an online certificate, and now he can testify as an expert in that field. Then after attacking his credibility on that, I go through what he currently just told the jury and I explain "So, because you just told this jury X, Y, and Z, this particular product is not worth anything. Isn't that true?" He will say yes. Then I go back and I pull up the transcripts that I've already researched and pulled out from his previous cases and I say, "Okay, do you remember in 2006, in the case of so and so versus so and so, where you were hired as an expert on the plaintiff?" He has to remember it. If he doesn't, then I can show him the case because I've pulled up the transcript and I say, "In that case you testified, because of the same exact reasons, the same X, Y, or Z, the product was worth $5 million to $10 million," whatever value he put on the product in that case.

Then I go through another case and another case, where he uses the same thing and the same analysis, to show he is swapping it around, to attack his credibility. The next step on cross examining expert witnesses once again, do not get into the technicality of their expertise. Don't attack it. You are just going to be asking questions that you already know the answers to. Then, with regards to their expert testimony, you look at their deposition, and do the same line and page that you did with the cross exam of the defendant or the party. However, you look for things that they did not do. For example, one of the questions in your deposition should be, "in coming to your conclusions, what are the steps that you took?" He will go through 1, 2, 3, and 4… I researched online, "I went out to the scene and I talked to 20 people," and you make sure, "it's all you've done and nothing else, correct?" Yes.

Then when you talk to your experts in prepping for the cross examination of their experts then you say, "Okay. This is what he did. What other things should he have done?" Your expert will tell you he didn't do this and this, and so on. The things he did not do or he should have done. Then you ask them, in the cross examination, about the steps they did not take, but should have taken. "Did you do this and this?" If he says he did then you go back and you read the transcript. "Remember when I asked you what you did? You said one through seven and when I asked you if that was it, you said yes. Are you sure you said yes, and now all of a sudden a year later you are telling a jury another thing." So, you attack his credibility with regards to what he did not do. Same thing with his qualifications, you go back and you look at your expert's qualifications on that specific field versus his qualification.

If your expert has not received extra certificates or other education then you ask him, "Isn't it true that you don't have this specific certification? Isn't it true that you didn't do this specific study?" All you are doing is asking yes or no questions. These help when your expert gets on the stand, to testify he has these certificates or credentials, so you are attacking what he did not do. First you go through them to confirm the steps that he did not do, and the credentials that he does not have. Then you attack their credibility as to how often they have testified in court, and how many times they have testified. Another question you ask and ensure you have the answer, from his deposition previously, how much he charges, how much he has been paid so far for this case, and that gives him motive. If he has been charging $1000 an hour, and has already been paid $35,000 and you ask him how much more is owed, probably $10,000 to $12,000 is still owed.

Overall, he is getting paid $30,000 to $45,000 for his testimony. Then you ask if he has ever worked with opposing counsel before. Have you ever testified for him before? How did you hear about him? Because that shows his income source if the other side hires him frequently on cases. If he testifies as to things that are not beneficial to the other side, then they are not going to hire him anymore. That's also benefitting you in your cross examination. You establish what he did not do, you establish how much he was paid, you establish his credentials and how he is not qualified, and then you establish further how much income he makes on an annual basis from testifying in court, versus any other source of income that he has. For some of these experts, it's 100% of what they do for income.

All they do is testify, which helps out the case on your end, and it's how he puts food on the table. Some doctors, for example, testify about 30% to 40% of the time and actually practice 50% to 60% of the time. For that also, you do the math and say, "Okay, 40% of the time. So how much income on an annual basis are you getting with regards to testifying, and he will tell you approximately $200,000 a year. You use that later with regards to, once again, motive to be bias, and motive to testify on the other side's behalf, because of the fact that $200,000 a year is coming from their testimony.

One of the key skills of cross-examining is to be able to think on your feet. No matter how much you prepare, you will be surprised by some of the answers by witnesses, and you need to be able to think on your feet to have good follow up questions. Sometimes you need to let the witness think you know more than you know, or you have more evidence than you really do. This will push them to tell the truth if they think you are going to catch them in a lie.

For example, if I have a witness on the stand and I have caught them a few times lying to the jury, and I have pointed it out on his/her deposition. I might, on the fly, look at the deposition, pretend that I am reading from there and ask a question that is damaging to the witness, but since I have them in a flow, and they think it's in their depo, they might just give me that answer and say Yes. If I get the answer I am looking for, I move on, and don't mention it again.

Another good example is when I had a case where I was cross-examining the defendant's expert, and he was so frustrated with the way the questions were going, he gave me a ridiculous response that did not make sense. It was a case regarding the value of a patent and he said he had worked with many companies who spent millions of dollars on products without ever receiving patents. This was obviously not true, and I knew it, but had not prepared for it. I was very surprised that he had said this, so I said, "Are you telling us that you have worked with many companies who have spent millions on products with no patents?" He said yes, it's not uncommon. At this point, what he did not know was that the courthouse had no internet access, I had my co-counsel sitting at the desk with a laptop in front of him, and I pointed to the laptop and said, "Can you please give us the name of one of those companies so we can look them up right now?" The witness got very nervous at this point and said, "Well I can't think of one at this point." My response was, "you just told this jury that you knew of many companies that do this, and you can't even think of one? Is that what you are telling us?" He could not, because he knew he would be caught in the lie, so he said "No I can't think of one now." I then knew I had him. He had no idea, that my co-counsel at that point was staring at a blank screen, because we had no internet access. Sometimes you need to bluff and if you do it convincingly, the witness will open up because they are afraid of being caught in their lies.

This is something you need to be ready for on cross- examination. You must be able to think on your feet and be ready for the witnesses to lie, and try to get away with it.

CHAPTER 10

CLOSING ARGUMENTS IN A TRIAL

The closing arguments and the cross examination of the witness are, in my opinion, the most fun part of the trial. This is where you have the opportunity to argue, this is where you show your passion for your clients, and where you show the jury how you feel about the case. You can open up and talk to them, with no concern of holding back, as I mentioned, one of my favorite parts of the trial. In closing arguments, as in the opening, I try to print out the opening from the opposing side, and go through the evidence to see what they did not prove that they said they would in the opening. What promises did they make? I read over those transcripts and highlight each one.

The next thing I do is get the jury instructions. A lot of people don't use jury instructions in their closing arguments. I like using these to give me authority, because the judge will read the jury these laws again, before they are dismissed. I like to put that up on the projector and use as many of the jury instructions that I can in my closing. So, in preparation of my closing arguments, I get the transcripts, I get the jury instructions that apply, and I use those in my closing. You can argue here what your case is worth, you make the demand of what your case is and why you are there, and you make sure that you follow the theme. Now, during the trial, it is very important, like during jury selection opening, to make eye contact with the jury when you are talking to them in voir dire or jury selection, and little notes they took from what they said, and put those notes in your closing arguments.

For example, if during jury selection one of the jury members made a statement with regards to "in order for me to provide $10 million in value to a case, I need the experts to be extra sure about the damages or other tangible proof," I might use that specific term during my cross of that expert. Then, in closing, make that argument and make eye contact with that specific jury member, and let him know that an expert testified and he was so sure about that X, Y, or Z. I look at him directly when I'm making that statement saying, "Remember how in jury selection you said that it was an issue? Well I answered your question. I think I passed that hurdle and we should get the damages because of that. Correct?"

I always take little notes about what jurors said during jury selection, and I try, in my theme during the trial, if at least one or two jurors say it, take notes to prove what they are looking for. Another thing would be if, for example, during jury selection, someone says I don't believe paid doctors, they can say anything, then I want to use real doctors, treating doctors. So we bring in the treating doctors and I ask them during the direct with my doctor, "Are you a treating doctor or are you paid for your services here?" He will say I am a treating doctor, and that person is my patient, and I'm not making a dime. So when I'm making my closing, I look that juror in the eye and I say, "We presented to you a treating physician, we didn't pay them to show up. Their doctor gets paid $1000 an hour to get up and tell you this. Our doctor testified to what really happened. They care about the patient and actually treated the patient, and that's what we brought to you." I look them in the eye when I say that, and that's the connection.

In the beginning, the jurors will make statements to you. When you take good notes of that, get a transcription of the jury selection and review it. Then bring these up in your closing arguments, quick call outs to make connections with the jury members. Another really important part of closing arguments is to remember to make eye contact. When you are talking to them, don't sit down and read a closing argument. You are not here just to read, they are all going to fall asleep. Start looking at them and talk to them, and look them in the eye when you are saying it. One by one, you should make eye contact with all the jury members during your closing arguments at least once, maybe multiple times. That keeps them alert because they are thinking, "Oh my God, this guy is looking right at me." They can't fall asleep, they'll take notes and it gives you credibility when you are talking to them, because you are not talking at them, you are talking right to them and explaining your situation.

Use visual effects in your closing. I really like to use PowerPoint and especially, on a long trial, if it went on for 3 to 5 weeks, they are not really going to remember all the people that testified in the first 2-4 days of a trial. I'll bring up some pictures in PowerPoint. "Witness John Smith, here is his picture" and make points about what he testified to. In closing arguments, I bring up how in opening I told them the case is going to go and guess what? We presented it exactly that way and here is how. Witness A testified, Witness B testified, Witness C testified, show them a picture and recall what they said. Then I review how the defense or the other side did not prove their case, and I put up their pictures and now I attack their credibility. I put up the pictures of their experts and I attack their credibility by highlighting what they did not do, or why their numbers don't add up.

Next, I go through the jury instructions on the law, and why we need to use specific ones that apply and how they help our case. This is another good thing to do in the closing argument, because at the end of the day when the jury makes a ruling, they come out with what is called a special verdict form. It's a form that you, opposing counsel and the judge put together which says, for example, was the defendant negligent? Yes or no, and then you move to the next one, were there damages? Yes or no, and move to the next one, what are the damages? I put that on the board or the projector, and I explain to them what it means. I go through the page and I actually put the checkmarks for them the way that I think they should respond, how I think the evidence is going to show, and how the evidence did show. The reason I do that is it helps them when they're deliberating in the jury room. These questions may be wordy or confusing, and there are times the jury does not understand it. I explain each one to them, and secondly, sit down and put the X marks on the checkmarks where I think they should go. Was the defendant negligent or in breach of contract? Yes, and I literally put an X mark next to yes in front of everyone so they see it.

Then the next portion, was the defendant's conduct a significant factor of the plaintiff's injuries? Yes and I checkmark it, BIG **bold** on the screen for everyone to see. What are the defendant's damages? This is where I explain to the jury, "look, you are the voice of the community. You are going to tell us what the value of this case is. I have an understanding of what I think this case is worth, the defense has an understanding of what they believe their case is worth, but ultimately what you believe its worth is going to count. I have a duty to tell you what I think the case is worth, and I think it's worth $9 million." I would write the figure 9,000,000.000 and there is a reason for that. I want to make sure that it's written out and they see it and it's not shocking. It's okay to write that number with that many zeros and that many digits. I explain how I came up with that number.

Don't come up with a random number without explaining how, you need to give the jury examples. You tell them that in a personal injury case, there is no formula that I can give you which says 2 times 2 is 4. That is the answer, and because of that it's what the local community or we think the value of the injury this person has suffered is. I like to use an hourly basis to calculate the pain and suffering. I bring up the fact that they've used an expert, and they paid that expert $1000 an hour to testify on the stand in order to try to receive a discount on their damages, because if that expert knocks down a certain amount of their damages, that expert has done their job. For example, if my client testifies and the evidence shows in a personal injury case that 5 days a week, 10 hours a day, his knee is in so much pain that he can't walk. 10 hours a day, 5 days a week, even if you give him $50 an hour and do the math in front of them. $50 an hour times 10 hours a day is $500 a day, times 5 days a week is $2500 a week, times 52 weeks a year, times this has happened for the last 3 years, times this is going to happen for the rest of his life. Jury instructions say that if it's a female, females live to be 83 years old and this person is in her late twenties, so they have 60 years left, 60 times whatever that number is, and that's how I get to that $9 million. So I go through the numbers and explain it to them. The defense is going to come up with a random number but they are not going to be able to explain how they came to it, and I use that against them. Before finishing my closing argument, I always thank them for their time on behalf of my client and myself, and let them know the defense is going to make their arguments now.

Once the defense is finished with their closing, I will make my final rebuttal arguments and thank them. I tell them, "please hold the defendants to the same standards, to show you the number the defense counsel is going to give you. Have them show you how they came up with that number, so we can see what kind of value they are putting on the quality of life for my client." When you do that, now you are putting the pressure on them. 90% of the time, the other side is going to get up and give a random number. They are not going to listen to it. They are going to take it as an insult that I am telling them how to do their closing. They are going to say it's worth zero, which would be the biggest mistake in a personal injury case, or they'd say it's worth $10,000. Then when I do my rebuttal, I show them that I do the math. While they are simply giving a number, I do the math. They say give him only $50,000; instead of the $9 million.

I quickly do the math of what the hourly rate is. So for $50,000 divided by this many hours, this many times, this many years, they are putting a value of 5 cents an hour on my client's pain and suffering, or her human suffering and her loss. That's what they think her pain is worth. That's the value they are putting on it. I say exactly these words in my rebuttal. Always make sure, to show in your rebuttal, that the value the opposing party is putting on your client's pain and suffering. Make sure you know your client, spend some time with them, because during the rebuttal when you rebut all their presumptions that this case is worthless, and it has no reason for it to be here, you are talking about the person that is sitting there. He or she is not just a number, not just someone. They suffered and they are actually going through this and they are going to go through this for the rest of their lives.

If you know that person, if you talk to them, the passion that you present comes out. I go to my clients' house for dinner, I meet with their family, and I get to know them, because that cannot be faked. The other side has no idea who your client is, and the jury doesn't know them. You need to explain to them why this person's value is so high, why their life, their pain and their suffering should have a significant value, and to do that you need to know them. You need to know their families, you need to know who they spend their time with, what they do for fun, because then and only then can you present that to the jury and get full value for your clients pain and suffering.

CHAPTER 11

CASE IS FINISHED

Once the case is finished, you will have an opportunity to talk to the jury, and this is a great place to talk to them about how you presented your case. I like to ask them about how I should improve, many lawyers like to ask about what they did well, to boost their egos. I like to ask what I can do better next time? I get my ego boost by the verdicts, I don't need to hear how good I am at the end. I think even something as simple as one jury member once told me, "it was annoying when you wore these squeaky shoes to court." She said she did not like me that day. I made sure I found out which shoes it was and made sure never to wear those in court again.

Talk to them as long as they are willing to stay and talk to you. This is where you can grow as a trial lawyer. You will know what they actually talked about in that jury room. It is amazing the things that they tell you and how they came to form their ruling. Some of the reasons they come up with their conclusions do not make any sense to you as a lawyer, but you will be happy with the good result for your client.

I had a jury member tell me that he was focused on the way I was cross examining the medical expert and the way I was forming the questions, he knew where I was going with the questions and knew why I was asking them. He was on our side the rest of the trial.

You never know how a jury member reacts to what you say or how you say it. I have had jury members tell me after a victory that I annoyed them because I pushed a point too far, they had got the point and wanted me to move on. There is an art to it, and you only will know your strength and weaknesses by taking cases to trial. You only learn from being in the courtroom and talking to the jury and having opposing counsel object to your questions, and judges not paying attention and making bad rulings. You need to be out there and take the cases to trial in order to learn and create your own way of doing things.

If you only learn one thing from this book, I would say it should be taking your cases to trial, if you do, you will learn more about how you personally can-do certain things well and what you need to work on. You will learn how a jury reacts to you, and what you can do to improve the way you personally connect with the jury.

Good luck and keep learning from your mistakes and each time you will become a better trial lawyer.

INDEX

NOTES

Made in the USA
Monee, IL
05 November 2026

67378083R00062